THE WONDERFUL WORLD OF WORDS

Ariana Has a Funfair

Dr Lubna Alsagoff
PhD (Stanford)

Marshall Cavendish
Children

Ariana was feeling a little bored.

Like many people in WOW,
Ariana had caught a cold and
had lain in bed for many days.

Now that I am much better,
I must do something.

Ariana decided that she would do something very grand to help lift the spirits of everyone at WOW.

Ariana texted the king and queen.

I'd like to organise a WOW funfair, with lots of fun rides and food!

Great idea!

Can I have some soldiers to help me?

Of course!!

Ariana had all her friends help with the funfair, and soon the fair would be open.

Ariana wanted to thank the adverbs in the kingdom. So, she decided that on the first day, she would open the fair only to the adverbs.

That's a wonderful idea!

The adverbs had been very good to her especially when she was sick.

They came to visit her
_____ [lydia].

They cared for her
_____ [tdrleeny].

They worked _____
[lituqye] when she was asleep.

They had her laughing
_____ [heyrtail]
at their jokes!

HA!

HA!

HA!

They cooked all her meals
_____ [tufuldlyi].

They _____ [clrfeluyerh]
helped with chores around
the house.

5

On the day the fair opened, the adverbs woke up early and began queuing to get into the fair.

happily

I think this
will be fun!

grumpily

Why do we
have to queue?

We need to
have some order,
don't you think?

carefully

Let's just rush in!
The queue is
too slow!

hurriedly

When the other adverbs had gone in, there were some rather angry and frustrated adverbs still waiting.

But I'm an adverb! Why aren't you letting me in?

You don't have an *ly* ending.

Not all adverbs need to have *ly* endings!

I thought adverbs always end in *ly*.

Not always!

7

Can you spot which words are adverbs?
Circle them.

1. I need a very loud alarm clock
   to get me out of bed.

2. The shop that sells the chocolate pies
   usually has a long queue.

3. Elephants can move silently in the
   thick jungle.

4. The soldiers have almost finished
   cleaning the castle.

5. Weaver birds build nests
   that ingeniously hide their eggs.

Now match the adverbs you've found
to the words below. These words have the
same meanings as the adverbs you've found.

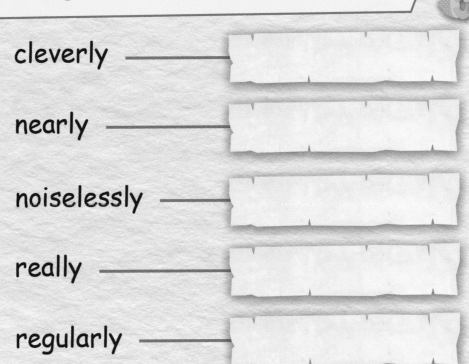

cleverly ⎯⎯⎯⎯⎯

nearly ⎯⎯⎯⎯⎯

noiselessly ⎯⎯⎯

really ⎯⎯⎯⎯

regularly ⎯⎯⎯⎯

Ariana gave the soldiers a little lesson on adverbs just in case more adverbs came along.

There are many adverbs that do not have *ly* endings. So, it's best not to just see how they look like.

HOW DO YOU SPOT AN ADVERB?

To check if a word is an adverb, find out what they do!

It is very well known that adverbs **help** verbs.

The queen **often** exercises in the park.

The king walked **slowly** along the garden path.

It is less well known that adverbs **help** adjectives.

The queen is **very** strong!

I am **almost** sure the princess has gone to the forest.

She must be **extremely hungry**.

And very few people know that adverbs sometimes help nouns.

The shops nearby are not open on Sundays.

The questions below must be answered.

And even fewer people know that adverbs can help quantifiers!

The bag weighed almost fifty kilograms!

Nearly half the people said they would eat chocolate for dinner!

And don't forget that adverbs also help other adverbs!

It's amazing how she does things so quickly!

Robbie very carefully put all the eggs in the basket.

Let's help the soldiers revise their adverbs!

The soldiers sat _____ and listened to Artisan Ariana.

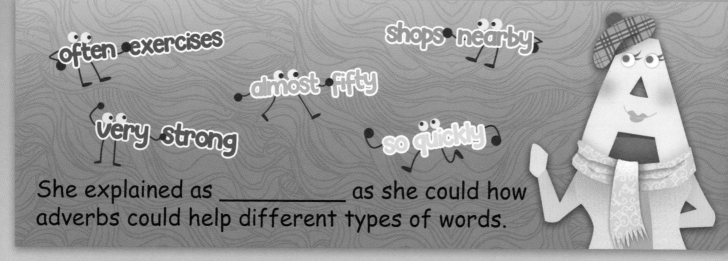

She explained as _____ as she could how adverbs could help different types of words.

Each soldier knew that it was _____ important that all the adverbs were allowed to go into the funfair on the opening day.

And they all wanted to do their _____ best to help Artisan Ariana.

_____ all the adverbs had already gone into the fair grounds, but they were waiting for the last ones to come.

King Noun and Queen Verb would _____ be arriving to join in the party.

Admiral Adjective would _____ be coming as well.

_____ the Count was coming!

Once everyone had arrived, the soldiers could _____ go to the fair!

Outside, some rather cheeky adjectives were planning to sneak into the party. They were adjectives that looked a lot like adverbs!

I'll go in first, everyone likes me!

Hello, adverb! You're quite late for the party.

Yes, I am! Please let me in.

Wait a minute, are you an adverb?

Can't you see my *ly* ending?

What sort of work do you do?

Mrs Hippo was sitting in class waiting for Mr Hippo.

We can wait a few minutes for Mr Hippo.

Just as Owl was about to start class, Mr Hippo rushed into the classroom huffing and puffing.

Owl had been listening to Mr and Mrs Hippo argue.
He decided to help.

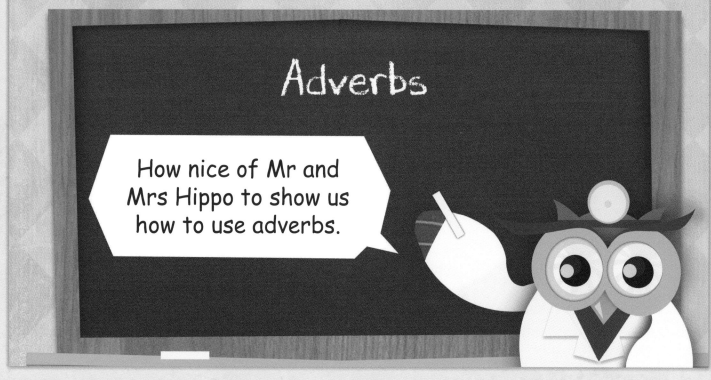

How nice of Mr and Mrs Hippo to show us how to use adverbs.

Adverbs can help us describe how frequent or how often something happens.

Is Mr Hippo always late?

I'm sorry, perhaps I should have said that Mr Hippo is frequently late or usually late.

I think he's late most of the time for class.

Perhaps I am often late!

I think you are sometimes late for class, Mr Hippo. You were only late for two classes. And we've had twelve classes.

Well then, I think we should say that Mr Hippo is seldom late.

And I shall try never to be late from now on!

Owl wrote the adverbs that the animals used:

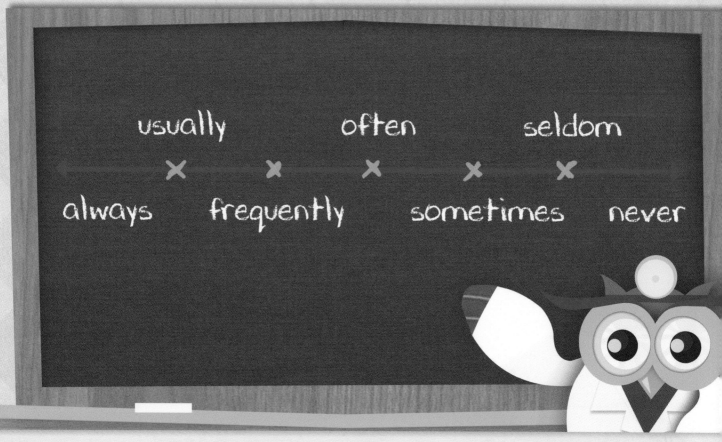

Help the animals practise writing sentences with these adverbs.

I must _____ leave early so I won't be late.

I _____ wake up at 7 am but today I overslept.

I _____ forget to put the cap back on the toothpaste.

My mother says we must _____ lie.

I like the big shady tree in WOW Park, so I _____ sit on its biggest branch to eat my lunch.

When the animals had finished, Princess Preposition came into the classroom.

Owl had invited her to tell the animals about adverbs.

The princess told the animals about how Admiral Adjective and Artisan Ariana played a game. The admiral would toss Ariana an adjective and she would turn it into an adverb.

sweet

nice

careful

sweetly

nicely

carefully

Sometimes the admiral would try a tricky adjective, but Ariana would know she could not turn all adjectives into adverbs with an *ly*.

For adjectives that end in y

happy → happi

clumsy → clumsi

ready → readi

For adjectives that end in e

comfortable → comfortab

clumsy → clumsi

ready → readi

And we must not forget that we have some spelling rules!

Dear Parents,

In this volume, we learn a little more about adverbs. Adverbs are usually identified by the *ly* endings but children need to know that there are many adjectives that also have *ly* endings.

The animals in WOW Forest also help to show children how to use frequency adverbs to accurately describe how often events and actions happen and learn about how some adverbs are formed from adjectives.

Page	Possible Answers
5	daily | tenderly | quietly | heartily | dutifully | cheerfully
9	very | usually | silently | almost | ingeniously

cleverly ⟶ ingeniously
nearly ⟶ almost
noiselessly ⟶ silently
really ⟶ very
regularly ⟶ usually

Page	Possible Answers
12–13	quietly | slowly | most | very | almost | soon | also | even | finally
20-21	always | usually | sometimes | never | often